The text of this book is set in Garamond.
ISBN 978-0-547-91416-9
Manufactured in China
LEO 10 9 8 7 6 5 4 3 2
4500403040

MARGRET AND H. A. REY'S

Where Is Curious George?

A LOOK AND FIND BOOK

WRITTEN BY CYNTHIA PLATT

ILLUSTRATIONS IN THE STYLE OF H.A. REY BY GREG PAPROCKI

HOUGHTON MIFFLIN HARCOURT

BOSTON   NEW YORK

Way up high in a tree,

Little house sits happily.

See that ladder? Up he'll stride!

George is curious: What's inside?

In the tree house, tiny spaces.

These are special kinds of places!

Find a crayon, find a chair,

Superhero, fuzzy bear,

Picture that your best friend drew.

Are you curious? I am too.

Where is George?

Standing tall amid the fields.

Look! That tractor has huge wheels!

Smell of hay is in the air.

George steps in to meet the mare.

In the red barn, sheep are baa-ing,

Chickens peck, and goats
are maa-ing.

Find a shovel, find a pig,

Find a wagon wheel that's big!

Milking pail to help milk Bessie . . .

My, oh my, this place is messy!

Where is George?

Nestled in a forest green,

Smallest cabin ever seen!

Up the pathway, open door.

George is curious: What's in store?

Crowded cabin, rough-and-tumble.

Whoops! Be careful—
you might stumble!

Find a kettle, find a can,

Downy quilt, frying pan.

A very tiny golden key.

Oh, that monkey—where is he?

Where is George?

My, how cozy this place feels!

It's a house that runs on wheels.

Step right in, head inside—

George is going for a ride!

Jam-packed trailer, lots to see

In a house that's wild and free.

Find a toothbrush, find a plate,

Old blue surfboard, roller skate.

Map for driving to and fro.

Tell me: Where'd that monkey go?

Where is George?

Warm brown door, sun-baked clay,

In the desert this house lay.

Orange colored, windows square.

George is curious—what's in there?

In the pueblo, windows small,

Nice designs upon the wall.

Find a dog bed, find a mug,

Find a painted water jug.

Wide-brimmed hat that
gives off shade.

Now where has that
monkey strayed?

Where is George?

Half on land, half at sea,

Rising up for all to see.

Stilts to make it safe from tides—

Through the door this
monkey strides!

In the stilt house, way up high—

Like you're living in the sky.

Find a seashell, find a shawl.

Kayak mounted on a wall.

Fishing rod to catch a snack.

Wish that monkey
would come back!

Where is George?

On a rocky crop at sea,

This house stands out mightily.

High wind rocks you as it blows.

George is curious—there he goes!

In the lighthouse, lantern lights

Guide the ships on stormy nights.

Find the flashlight, find the boots,

Coat that makes you waterproof.

Telescope to see out far.

George, I wonder where you are!

Where is George?

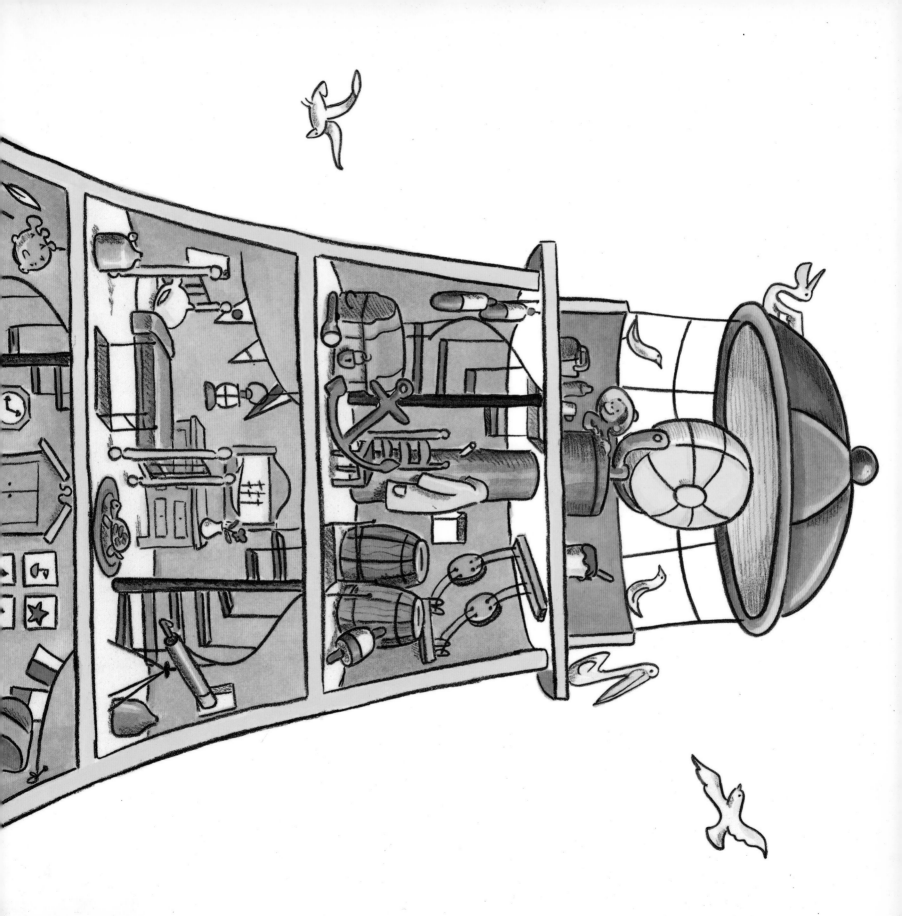

Step on board, if you please!

This house sails the seven seas.

On the deck—saw a fin!

Are you curious? What's within?

On the houseboat, floor is moving

To the ocean's endless grooving!

Find a compass, find a rope,

Binoculars, a bar of soap.

Life jacket to keep you floating.

Still, I'm curious: Is George boating?

Where is George?

Walls are lofty, made of stone.

Knights and ladies call it home.

Flags are flying, towers soaring—

George is curious! Let's go touring.

Castle regal, ceilings tall,

Torches hung upon each wall.

Find the candle, find the sword,

Knight's strong shield,
orange gourd.

Ruby in a golden crown.

Look for monkey, up and down.

Where is George?

Monkey see, monkey do—

monkey house inside the zoo!

Rainforest inside this gate.

George is curious—
just can't wait!

Tall palm trees in the ground,

Lots of creatures all around!

Find a toucan, find a swing.

Find a toy plane, find three rings.

Coconuts hanging from a tree.

Now just where is our monkey?

Where is George?

Rising high into the clouds,

Big enough to hold a crowd.

Take an elevator ride—

George is curious: What's inside?

Huge skycraper, tall and bustling.

Lots of people, lots of hustling!

Find a scooter, find two puppies,

Find a tank that's filled
with guppies.

Calendar, and pillow round.

Where, oh where, can
George be found?

Where is George?

Home sweet home! Happiness!

There's no place that's
quite like this.

Two steps up—come right in!

Someone's wondering
where you've been.

In his house this monkey swings,

Looking round for all his things.

Find a bunny, find a kite.

Yum, bananas! Lamp that's bright.

Yellow hat fit for a friend—

At a monkey journey's end!

Where is George?